Citizenship

Being Helpful

Cassie Mayer

CAPSTONE PRESS
a capstone imprint

www.capstonepub.com
Visit our website to find out
more information about
Heinemann-Raintree books.

To order:
☎ Phone 888-454-2279
🖳 Visit www.capstonepub.com
    to browse our catalog and order online.

© 2008 Heinemann Library
a division of Capstone Global Library, LLC.
Chicago, Illinois

www.mycapstone.com

Designed by Joanna Hinton-Malivoire
Illustrated by Mark Beech

The Library of Congress has cataloged the first edition of this book as follows:
Mayer, Cassie.
 Being helpful / Cassie Mayer.
     p. cm. -- (Citizenship)
 Includes bibliographical references and index.
 ISBN 978-1-4846-4891-9 (pbk.)
 1. Helping behavior--Juvenile literature. I. Title.
 BF637.H4M39 2007
 177'.7--dc22
                          2006039386

Table of Contents

Being helpful means giving
a hand.

Being helpful means thinking of others.

When you help carry things ...

you are being helpful.

When you wash the dishes …

you are being helpful.

When you watch after your
sister ...

you are being helpful.

When you put away toys ...

you are being helpful.

When you follow instructions ...

you are being helpful.

When you look out for others ...

you are being helpful.

When you ask what you can do ...

you are being helpful.

Being helpful is important.

How can you be helpful?

Activity

How is this child being helpful?

Picture Glossary

being helpful give people help when they need it

instruction written or spoken list of how to do something

Index

Note to Parents and Teachers
Each book in this series shows examples of behavior that demonstrate good citizenship. Take time to discuss each illustration and ask children to identify the helpful behavior shown. Use the question on page 21 to ask students how they can be helpful to people in their lives.

The text has been chosen with the advice of a literacy expert to enable beginning readers success while reading independently or with moderate support. You can support children's nonfiction literacy skills by helping them use the table of contents, picture glossary, and index.